# People of Destiny

*A Humanities Series*

*There comes a time,*
*we know not when,*
*that marks*
*the destiny of men.*

Joseph Addison Alexander

*People of Destiny*

# POPE JOHN XXIII

*By Norman Richards*

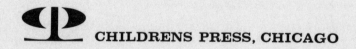 CHILDRENS PRESS, CHICAGO

*The editors wish to express
their appreciation to Mr. Meyer Goldberg,
who created the series and inspired
the publication of* People of Destiny.

*Cover and body design: John Hollis*

*Project editor: Joan Downing*

*Assistant editor: Elizabeth Rhein*

*Illustrations: John Downs, Ron Kangles
—Hollis Associates*

*Research editor: Robert Hendrickson*

*Photographs: From the files of Wide
World Photos, Inc.*

*Typesetting: American Typesetting Co.*

*Printing: Regensteiner Press*

*Library of Congress Catalog Card No. 68-31307*

2 3 4 5 6 7 8 9 10 11 12 13 14 15 16 17 18 19 20 21 22 23 24 25  R  75 74 73 72 71 70 69

# Contents

# Toward Christian Unity

The dark, forbidding sky and the cold rain in Rome on October 11, 1962, could not dampen the enthusiasm of the thousands of church officials who had gathered in that city. A rare event was taking place at the Vatican, the ancient seat of the Roman Catholic church. Pope John XXIII, Vicar of Christ, spiritual head of the church and temporal head of the Vatican State, had summoned an Ecumenical Council. Not since 1869 had a pope called for such a meeting; officials of the church throughout the world who held the rank of bishop or higher would come together to discuss problems and crises within the worldwide church. But the 1962 Ecumenical Council would be radically different from previous councils.

Throughout his "career" in the church, Pope John XXIII had dreamed of improving communication and bettering relations between the Roman Catholic church and the other Christian churches. For hundreds of years the various Christian denominations in the world had gone their separate ways, distrusting one another. Although they all believed in the divinity of Christ, each had a different way of worshiping and a different organizational structure. Too often, when they should have been concentrating on the things they had in common, they were arguing about their differences. This negative attitude toward cooperation with each other had prevented Christians from working together toward common goals.

As head of the largest Christian church, Pope John had decided to take the initiative and begin a specific program with a goal of bringing about a new era of understanding and cooperation among Christians. Most people thought the Pope's ultimate goal of Christian unity was unattainable. It was this kind of negative, divisive thinking that he hoped to change.

Whatever Pope John did to promote his views, however, he could not radically depart from the traditional actions of popes before him. But as head of the Roman Catholic church he could bring thousands of influential Catholic clergymen together and instruct them to take a new, more pro-

gressive attitude toward cooperation with other churches. He could also invite representatives of other churches to attend this meeting as observers, thereby impressing them with the urgency and sincerity of his plea for unity and cooperation. And so he decided to convene an Ecumenical Council.

The Pope first publicized his idea for the council nearly four years before the council actually began. This action, coming as it did only three months after his elevation to the papal throne, confirmed the fact that Pope John had no desire to be simply an "interim pope"— one whose reign would be fairly short and would serve as a bridge between the reigns of two younger, more active popes. But Pope John XXIII, throughout his reign, never ceased to surprise those around him, not only in calling for the council but in his efforts to be closer to the people whose spiritual father he was. He succeeded so well that he has become one of the best-loved popes in history.

The Pre-Preparatory Committee of the council sent out hundreds of questionnaires to churchmen all over the world. The men were asked to tell what church-related problems they considered important. The responses to these questionnaires were then sorted and published in fifteen volumes.

The Pre-Preparatory Committee then set up fifteen committees which would be the organizational base of the council. Each of these committees was headed by a cardinal or an archbishop, with the central committee headed by the Pope himself. The individual committees had topic assignments. One committee might have bishops and dioceses, while another would be studying Oriental churches. All of these topics were matters which had received a great deal of comment in the questionnaires. Each committee studied all phases of its assigned topic, and the findings served as the basis for the council's agenda.

After forty-five months of this preparation, including the planning necessary for an influx of 10,000 people into Rome and the Vatican for the council, all was ready. A great crowd of people gathered in St. Peter's Square that day in 1962 to watch the bishops of the church walk in procession from the Hall of Benedictions to St. Peter's Basilica, where the meetings would be held. All who saw the procession were deeply moved by its splendor and majesty.

First to appear was a group of the church's Palatine Guard, resplendent in their blue and gold uniforms. White-robed bishops who had come from all over the world followed them in row upon row as bands played marches and the people cheered.

The procession seemed to flow endlessly. Bishops of the Catholic Eastern Rite wore brilliant gold and purple robes and golden crowns. The sight of so many bishops and so much grandeur left the people who were watching the parade staring in awe and wonder.

Next came the eighty-two Roman Catholic cardinals, followed by the nine patriarchs of the Eastern Rite. Then came Pope John himself. He was borne high over the heads of the spectators in the famous litter of the popes. The men carrying it grasped long horizontal poles which rested on their shoulders. It looked like a beautiful golden throne with a canopy.

The cheers of the crowd reached a crescendo at the sight of the Pontiff, and the church bells rang. Though Pope John was known to be a sentimental man, easily moved by emotion, his face did not betray his strong feelings on this day, a momentous occasion both in his own life and in the history of the church.

*Top, Pope John engages in informal conversation with Francis Cardinal Spellman of New York (right) and James Cardinal McIntyre (left). Bottom, the Pope talks with Methodist bishop Fred P. Corson of Philadelphia (center).*

The nave of St. Peter's had been richly decorated. Thousands of seats had been installed which rose in tiers from the floor. Pope John had insisted that the observers—the non-Roman Catholics—be placed in the first rows, near the papal throne, to emphasize that they were welcome and important guests. There was no mistaking the Pope's sincere happiness that they had come.

The Pope sat on the high crimson and gold throne and the Sistine Choir sang *Veni Creator Spiritu*. Mass was celebrated, and later, people around the world were inspired by the Pope's sincerity and earnestness when he read the Confession of Faith. Millions of people throughout the world heard his words, for he had permitted live television coverage of the ceremony so that as many as possible could share in it. When he stood to give his blessing, people in many parts of the world knelt wherever they were.

Then the Pope began to read his address. He spoke fervently of the need for the church's methods to be adapted to modern times in order to reach people to whom its traditional ways seem irrelevant in the twentieth century.

He disagreed with pessimists who say the world is getting worse and expressed an optimism about man's chances to improve himself and become nearer to God. He spoke of new opportunities for the church to help people and to spread Christ's message.

He pointed out that the Doctrine of Faith must be presented in such a way that people can accept and apply it in the context of their lives. The council, he said, was not called to discuss specific doctrinal problems, but to make possible a more up-to-date system of thought. And he spoke of his great hope for unity among Christians, regardless of their church affiliations. He likened the council to the dawn of a new day, in which many outdated attitudes among Christians would be replaced by a new spirit transcending denominational differences.

Indeed, it was a new day in the history of Christianity, for Pope John set in motion a great many changes in his church. Like a chain reaction, many more changes came about, along with greater and greater cooperation among all Christians. Masses are said in local languages all over the world today, rather than in Latin, so that the worshipers can better understand them. Catholics and Protestants attend each other's religious services. Priests and ministers cooperate toward the common goals of Christianity in a way that seemed impossible not too many years ago. The feeling of charity, tolerance, and hope promises to result in even greater unity in the future.

It took a very special sort of man to set in motion the changes that would break down centuries-old barriers and prejudices among Christians. Only a man such as Pope John XXIII, whose genuine love for all his fellow men reached across the boundaries of suspicion, could have inspired this major change in men's minds and hearts.

His life prepared him for this role of destiny—from his peasant birth, through his distinguished career as one of the church's best diplomats, to the moment when this warm, loving man became head of Christianity's largest church and a source of inspiration to people everywhere.

*Top, Pope John blesses the crowd in St. Peter's Square at the opening of the Ecumenical Council. Bottom, the Pope addresses newsmen who would be reporting on the council. Left, the Papal Chamberlain. Right, Msgr. Salvatore Capoferri, master of pontifical ceremonies.*

# A Peasant Birth

Sotto il Monte is a little village located in Bergamo, in the north of Italy. Its name means "under the mountain," and this describes the town's location at the foot of some of northern Italy's lofty mountains near Lake Como.

On this day the November wind howled and whipped about a four-family house on the Via Brusicio in Sotto il Monte, and the rain sounded against the house's old, plain walls. Inside, there was a tiny room where the dampness and coldness of the rain had seeped. It was not a cozy room—the floor was red brick and the walls were worn with age and pockmarked with peeling plaster. The room contained a bed as its only piece of furniture. In the bed, covered by every blanket, rug, and spread available in the house, were Maria Anna Mazzola Roncalli, and her newborn son.

Signora Roncalli was a sturdy peasant woman who didn't mind the discomfort of her surroundings. Nearly everyone else in the little town lived in the same state of poverty—it was the way they had always lived. They cared little about fine clothes, houses, and fancy food. Their occupation was farming, and the hard farm work they did gave them ravenous appetites that were satisfied by meals of soup, cheese, bread, and pasta. They were happy people who felt their religion deeply and went to Mass every day, secure in their love of God.

The year was 1881, long before electric lights, radios, television, and automobiles would be seen in rural towns of Europe or America. The great majority of rural people had fewer comforts and a far lower standard of living than millions can enjoy even today.

The late nineteenth century was a time of empire building, and Great Britian was leading the way. Queen Victoria was at the height of her long reign, and the British Empire was being extended into Africa. Holland, Belgium, Portugal, Germany, and France

*Signora Maria Anna Mazzola Roncalli lies in bed with her newborn son. The two of them were protected from the cold and damp of the small house by every covering available.*

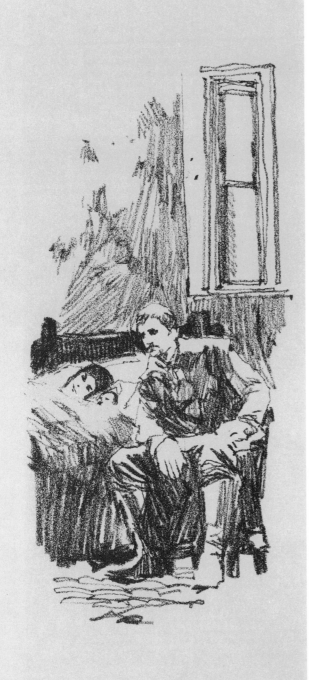

also were carving empires in Africa. India was under British rule and China was divided into small "kingdoms" under feuding rulers.

The United States of America was fast growing into a powerful country with the settlement of vast areas of the west and a growing industrialization. Railroads were tying the huge nation together for the first time and making industrial expansion easier. Thomas Edison was working with a new marvel called the incandescent lamp, and wondering how enough electricity to light an entire city could be produced and transported. Henry Ford had left the family farm in Michigan and was repairing watches for a living while trying to build an engine for a "horseless carriage." A young boy named Douglas MacArthur, son of a career army officer, would someday stamp his name in history as a great military leader.

But life for the peasants of Italy remained the same as it had been for centuries. The great wave of industrialization would not hit rural Italy until the twentieth century, when many of the young people would leave the farms and small towns for industrial cities.

The infant death rate was very high, for the causes of many diseases were unknown and the susceptible newborn could not be protected against them. There were no doctors or hospitals in most small towns. For this reason priests urged parents to have their infants baptized as soon as possible. Thus, despite the cold, wet weather,

Signora Roncalli and her husband bundled up their hours-old son and prepared to walk to the village church to have him baptized. With them was Zaverio Roncalli, Signor Roncalli's uncle and head of the family. He was to be named the baby's godfather.

When the dripping trio of adults and the well-bundled infant arrived at the little church, they learned that the priest was in Terno, a nearby village, where he was visiting someone who was ill. Though the Roncallis did not know how long he would be gone, they sat down silently and waited for him to return.

It was more than four hours later when the priest, Father Rebuzzini, finally swung the door open and escaped the rain and howling wind outside. He was tired and wet, and more than anything else he wanted to rest and spend a quiet evening alone. He suggested that the Roncallis might come back the next day, but when he saw the disappointment in their faces he agreed to baptize the baby right away.

The small bedraggled group went to the damp, empty chapel where the child was baptized and named Giuseppe Angelo Roncalli, though the first two names were later inverted. The godfather, holding the child, went to the altar of the Madonna and placed the baby under her protection.

Because of the cold, the priest conducted the ceremony rapidly. When it was over the Roncallis walked home through the rain with the baby Angelo, happy that he had been baptized a Roman Catholic on the day of his birth. None of them could imagine that many years later this same child would rise to such an eminent position.

# A Priest in the Making

Bergamo, the area of Italy where Sotto il Monte is located, was not a bad place for a poor boy to grow up, even in the 1880's and 1890's. The countryside is beautiful in the warmer seasons of the year, and the mountain breeze is invigorating and fresh.

Angelo Roncalli's parents were certain at first that he would grow up to be a farmer like the other peasant people of the area. After all, his father had worked the land for many years and managed to provide for his family. He had even bought a large old house and some acreage of his own by the time Angelo was of school age. The family seldom had any cash, but they led a happy, healthy life. Ambitions extending beyond the confines of the village seemed so unlikely to be realized that the people of Sotto il Monte scarcely considered them.

Sotto il Monte had no school of its own, so the Roncallis sent Angelo to the school at Carvico, about a mile away, when he was six. He walked the entire distance barefooted, and like the other youngsters he would stop and play during the walk home each day, even in bad weather. When his father enrolled the youngster he told the priest to beat Angelo if he refused to study. The schoolteacher took Angelo's father literally, so the boy's introduction to education was a rough one. The harassed teacher, who had three classes of boys of all ages, often felt it necessary to pound their lessons into the youngsters, boxing their ears if they made a mistake.

Angelo was intelligent and should have had no difficulty in mastering his studies. But he loved to play more than he loved to study. Although he did not

*Angelo is shown here walking to school at Carvico. Though this town was about one mile away from Sotto il Monte, it had the closest school available. Angelo stopped and played along the road each day on the long walk home.*

19

show any signs of becoming a good student, Angelo learned to love reading. He enjoyed it so much that within three years he had read everything in the small school library. When his mother learned of this she beamed with pride. She even prayed that her son might not become a farmer, but instead continue his education and someday become a priest. This profession was just about the only acceptable alternative available to a peasant boy from a small Italian village.

Angelo, too, began to think of this ambition. Years later he recalled that at a very early age he decided that the thing he wanted most in the world was to become a priest.

In 1890, when he was nine, the boy's parents decided to send him to school in the San Marino Valley, about three miles away on the other side of a mountain. The school, called the Catholic College (though it was really an elementary school), was located in the town of Celano.

Again Angelo had to walk barefooted to school, but now he had three times as far to walk. He often trudged along the dirt road reading as he went, since walking six miles a day cut into his study time and tired him out, although he was a rugged, healthy boy. His grades, never high, began to reflect the time spent traveling to and from school. One of his report cards showed a failing mark in arithmetic and a slightly below average grade in four other subjects. There was certainly nothing there to indicate a brilliant future for this youngster.

Nevertheless, he passed the entrance examination and was accepted as a student at the seminary in the nearby city of Bergamo when he was eleven. In those days the seminary was one of the few places of higher education, and not all students there necessarily went on to become priests. They were, however, required to wear a cassock, a garment which has tight-fitting sleeves and hangs in loose folds to the ankles. These boys were fortunate to be allowed to study at the seminary, for few Italian children had an opportunity for higher education.

If Angelo thought that academic life was rugged at Celano, he was in for a much tougher routine at Bergamo. The hours were rigidly controlled at the seminary, with special times set aside for prayers and study. At least he could sleep at the school, though, and save the time he used to spend walking to and from school each day. More privileged boys found the seminary life almost too difficult to endure, but a sturdy, cheerful peasant boy like Angelo didn't find it unbearable at all.

The thought of becoming a priest spurred the youngster on. His attitude toward his studies became more serious,

and his grades improved. The more he dug into his studies the more interesting he found them, and before long his scholastic standing was very respectable. He especially liked history and philosophy, and he became intrigued with theology, poetry, and classical music.

Although his studies opened up to him a wider world of culture than his family had ever known, Angelo was first and foremost a peasant boy. He loved to travel the eight miles to Sotto il Monte to visit his family whenever he had free time, and he thoroughly enjoyed the simple pleasures of being with peasant people again. The cassock he wore as a student at the seminary awed his family when they first saw it, for in it he looked like a priest. Angelo was a bit embarrassed by this reaction, but his family soon saw that he was still the cheerful, peasant son in spite of his advanced learning.

Long after his mother had raised her hopes about her son becoming a priest, his father still had private doubts that Angelo would make it. The ambition had seemed too lofty for the son of a poor farmer. But as he saw his boy make steady progress at the seminary, he, too, became convinced that this child of his had enough determination to achieve his goal. Seeing Angelo in clerical garb heightened his imagination and his hopes.

On one of the visits home, Giovanni Roncalli walked into the fields with his son and suddenly stopped. Taking his spade, he shoved it into the earth repeatedly until the blade shone like silver in the sun. The spade was pointed, like a bishop's hat, and Giovanni looked at the shovel, then at Angelo.

"I hope I will live to see the day when you will wear the hat of a bishop," he said, and Angelo knew now that his father wanted this more than anything in the world. There were no longer any doubts or limited hopes.

Angelo moved further along the road to the priesthood when he was thirteen. He was given his first tonsure—that is, the rite of shaving his head to denote admission as a candidate for orders in the church. This took place on June 28, 1895. In the first year of the new century, which was to revolutionize civilization with tremendous progress in technology, Angelo Roncalli was graduated with honors from the seminary.

He had long since ceased to be a poor or even an average student, and his energy and brilliance caught the eye of the bishop of Bergamo. Sensing that the young student had the capability to advance in the church organization, the bishop presented him with a scholarship allowing him to study in Rome at the Seminario Romano, known at that time as the Apollinare. This was the finest school a would-be priest could enroll in, and only students of exceptional promise were admitted.

Young Roncalli was deeply honored by the appointment and made the trip to Rome with great expectations. When he arrived, however, he was taken aback because the building in which the Apollinare was located was big and dreary, and in the back streets of Rome. Angelo's room was tiny and damp. It had one barred window, making him think that living in a jail cell would be preferable. But none of this really made much difference to the boy, for he soon was swept up in the academic atmosphere.

*Above, Angelo's father makes his spade shine like a bishop's hat, signifying his desire that Angelo become a priest. Right, a portrait of Angelo's father.*

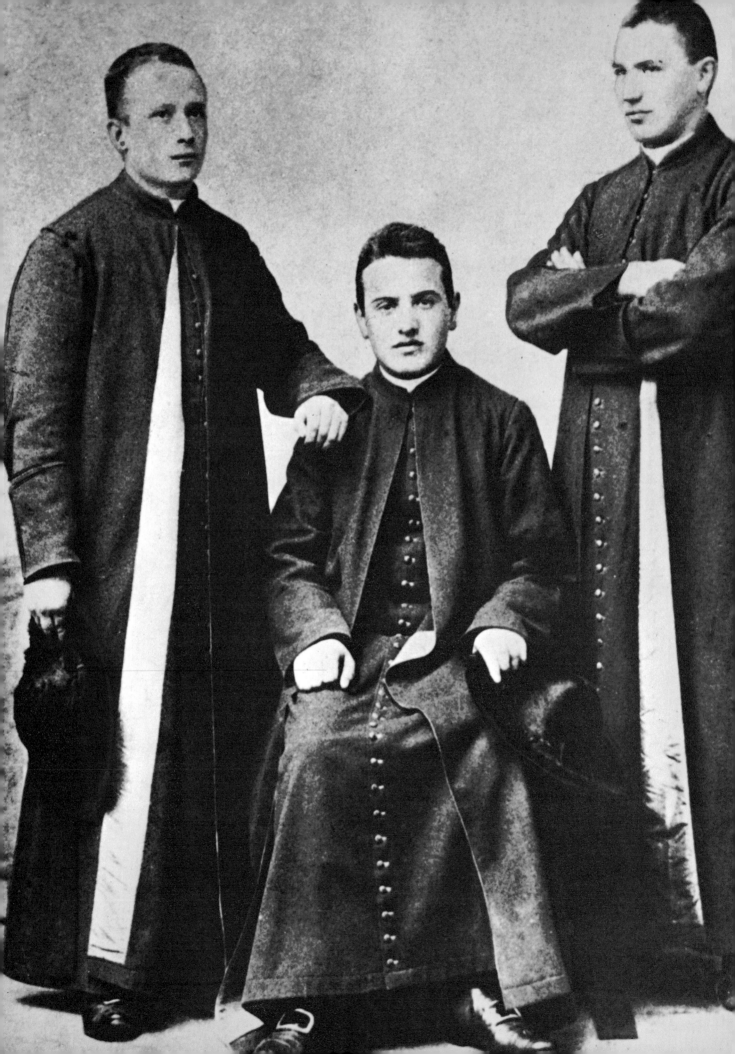

As a student in Bergamo, Angelo had finally begun to develop an interest in his studies. No longer was he the happy-go-lucky barefoot peasant boy who read voraciously but received barely passing grades. He had decided definitely that he would become a priest, and he worked steadily and tirelessly toward that goal. He became very fond of history, especially the history of the church itself. Though he did not do well in the sciences, he excelled at the humanities, possibly because of his great love and concern for people as individuals.

Now, at the Apollinare, he continued his study of church history and also became interested in canon law, a subject in which he did advanced work after he was ordained a priest. When he had time off from classes and studying he walked all over the ancient city with his classmates, thrilled with its timeless beauty and tradition of culture, and excited at the thought of being in the very home of the Roman Catholic church.

Seminary students were all expected to serve military duty. They had the right to volunteer for duty if they wished a certain regiment and wanted to finish their military service in one year.

Angelo Roncalli had been a student at the Apollinare for only a year when he received word that he was to serve his period of military duty. Obeying, he quickly joined the Seventy-third Infantry Regiment because it was stationed at Bergamo, near his home. He worked in the army with the same zest that he had displayed in his studies. He had little difficulty in feeling at home in army barracks life, although it was tougher for students from more luxurious backgrounds, as it had been at the school in Bergamo. After the long hours spent studying and living in his small cell at school, army life seemed almost like a holiday.

He wore his uniform with great pride, slanting his cap just a bit, and he was soon well-liked by the other soldiers. He looked every bit a soldier and not like a seminary student at all. Some of the friends he made during his year of military service remained close to him for the rest of his life. He had many opportunities during that year to visit his family in nearby Sotto il Monte, to their great joy.

The year passed quickly and Sergeant Roncalli was discharged to resume his studies at the Apollinare. In July, 1903, he was still studying in Rome when Pope Leo XIII died and he was witness to the solemn papal funeral and the thrill of an election of a new pope by the cardinals of the church.

After many days of voting, the conclave broke and the new pope was the Cardinal Patriarch of Venice, Giuseppe Sarto. Few had expected him to be elected. He was an excellent pope, though, and in fact was canonized a saint in 1950. He chose the name of Pius X.

On August 10, 1904, Angelo Roncalli was at last ordained a priest. He celebrated his first Mass the next day in St. Peter's Basilica. As he was leaving the basilica, the Pope himself appeared unexpectedly, and the new priest was thrilled at the opportunity to talk with the Holy Father. It was, he felt, the most wonderful first day as a priest that he could have imagined. But greater experiences lay ahead.

_____

*Angelo is shown with two unidentified fellow student priests. This photograph was taken in 1901, while Angelo was a student at the Apollinare.*

# God's Servant in War and Peace

August 15, 1904, was the proudest day the members of the large Roncalli family could remember. Their own kinsman, Don Angelo Roncalli, celebrated the Mass of the Assumption at the plain little church in Sotto il Monte where he had been baptized that rainy evening nearly twenty-three years before. He nervously gave his first sermon and afterward was warmly congratulated by everyone at the service. The townspeople were bursting with pride when Angelo returned to the Apollinare to study canon law and to become an assistant instructor.

He hadn't been in Rome long, however, when destiny stepped in to change his life in a way he never expected. Roncalli had always supposed he would become a simple country priest, administering to the needs of the type of people he had grown up with. But suddenly he was requested to embark in a different direction.

The Pope named Giacomo Maria Radini-Tedeschi, a brilliant member of the Holy See's organization, as bishop of Bergamo. He had served for many years as the Holy See's "public relations man" for Italy because of his great diplomatic ability. A man of strong opinions and a willingness to take unpopular stands if he believed in them, he had been a nobleman before giving up his high social position to enter the church. Pope Pius X thought so highly of Radini-Tedeschi that the Pope himself consecrated him. Two young priests from Bergamo assisted, one of whom was Roncalli.

The first thing the new bishop asked for was a secretary to aid him. He wanted a young man from Bergamo who knew and understood the people

*This photograph was taken in 1904 on the occasion of Angelo Roncalli's first mass, the Mass of the Assumption, said at Sotto il Monte.*

from that part of Italy, but one who had a good education in Rome and was not too provincial. He was especially considering the two young priests from Bergamo who had assisted at his consecration. The rector of the Apollinare, Monsignor Spolverini, to whom Radini-Tedeschi went for advice, concluded that Roncalli was the best qualified. He told the bishop that Roncalli had the unusual gift of being liked by nearly everyone, and also had a brilliant mind and a broad education. After an interview, Radini-Tedeschi was quickly convinced.

So the young priest suddenly found himself with a job at a high administrative level in the church, dealing with problems that were far more complex than those of a parish priest in a small village. It was a turning point in his life, but he did not question it, reasoning that it was God's will.

Roncalli quickly learned that his new post at Bergamo would be a demanding one, but one that would open up broad new experiences for him. One of his first missions was to accompany the bishop on a pilgrimage to Lourdes, the location of the grotto in France where the Virgin Mary had appeared to Bernadette. The experience of visiting Lourdes was deeply moving to Roncalli and the trip gave him his first exposure to a foreign country and a different way of life. The tolerance and understanding of other peoples that such trips would create were to be important in his long career in the church.

The pair traveled everywhere. The bishop was a tall, dignified man, in contrast to his assistant, the round, jovial Roncalli. The bishop soon discovered that his secretary was a very efficient hard worker who kept going no matter how little sleep he got. In turn, Roncalli deeply admired the brilliance of the man he served and found his convictions and willingness to stand by them inspiring. He came to love and admire this man as an example of greatness.

Radini-Tedeschi became bishop of Bergamo at a time when Catholics were beginning to reenter the political life of

*Roncalli and the bishop of Bergamo, Giacomo Maria Radini-Tedeschi, make a pilgrimage to the shrine of Lourdes in France, where Bernadette Soubirous had her vision of the Virgin Mary.*

their nation, after having been prohibited from participating in it for many years by decree of Pope Pius IX. Radini-Tedeschi wanted most of all to help Bergamo retain its reputation as one of the most Catholic cities in Italy. Before becoming a bishop, Radini-Tedeschi had been active in Catholic Action, the movement which was designed to band Catholic workers together in Catholic organizations to protect their interests and to give them a voice in their own future. In Bergamo, the bishop wanted to reorganize this movement, since it had long been plagued with dissension between two opposing groups within the organization. Radini's methods were so direct and to the point that he tended sometimes to incur the disfavor of his superiors. However, this did not matter much to him; his main concern was with accomplishing good things for the people in his diocese.

In 1909, a group of factory workers at Ranica, a suburb of Bergamo, went on strike. Workers had few rights in those days and strikes were rare. Bishop Radini-Tedeschi was one of the first people to agree to send money to aid the striking workers. This action shocked the industrial leaders and aristocrats, and the protests were long and loud. But Radini was convinced that the workers' cause was just, and he refused to yield. Finally the workers won their rights and went back to work, though newspapers continued to criticize the bishop for his stand.

After the bishop had taken his stand on the question of the striking workers, he and Roncalli watched and waited for reaction from Rome. Finally, Pope Pius X commended the bishop for the stand he had taken—he had been willing to submit to public criticism but would not surrender his principles.

This was just one of many examples through the years of how deeply the bishop cared for people and how brilliantly he accomplished the church's objectives. Roncalli's hero worship of the bishop grew, and in turn, the bishop's devotion to his loyal secretary increased until he loved him as he would a son. By example he taught him how the church's large organization could be used to help the people. Roncalli realized that he probably had the best teacher in the world.

The bishop organized the League of Women Workers in order to help employed women gain the same rights as men. He and Roncalli arranged to help thousands of workers travel to other countries to find jobs when times were hard in Italy. They also established an organization to give financial help to expectant mothers. Their work took them to many places, including Spain, France, and Palestine (now Israel), and Roncalli learned how the church was able to help people in different countries with different sets of problems.

*Striking factory workers in the suburb of Ranica are picketing in hopes of receiving better working conditions and wages. Bishop Radini-Tedeschi was one of the first to send money to these workers.*

This wonderful relationship lasted ten years before tragedy ended it. As time went on, Roncalli began to notice that his superior tired easily, even though he was not an elderly man. Radini-Tedeschi sought medical help as his health declined. It was discovered that he had cancer.

The lingering disease took its toll and the bishop grew weaker and weaker. By the summer of 1914, the cancer was spreading throughout his body and he was confined to his bed. As the end grew near, Radini and Roncalli talked together for long hours each day. A terrible sadness weighed upon Roncalli's mind, but he tried to hide it when he was with the bishop. Day after day Roncalli sat by his bedside in the darkened room as the bishop's life slowly ebbed away.

During this time, another sad event occurred. In August, Pope Pius X died and the church mourned the loss of its leader. Roncalli whispered the sad news to his bishop.

Bishop Radini-Tedeschi was silent for a moment and then told Angelo that when he had been consecrated a bishop, Pope Pius X had leaned over and whispered to him, "At your death I will come for you and we will be joined in paradise forever." Now the bishop smiled serenely, secure in the knowledge that he would join the Pope after death.

Two days later he died. His last words were those offering his life as a sacrifice

31

for the church, for the new pope, and then, in a very strong voice he added, "for peace in the world. . . ."

The death was a terrible blow to Roncalli, but the bishop's life had made a strong impression on his mind, and it was an example he followed for the rest of his life. A phase of his career was over, but he would never forget the bishop of Bergamo.

It was a sad time for people everywhere. Under the leadership of Kaiser Wilhelm, Germany had built a large army and together with its ally, Austria, was fighting France, Great Britain, Russia, and Italy. Countless thousands of young men were being killed on the battlefields. It was a new kind of warfare, for many modern weapons such as metal tanks, huge cannon, airplanes, and poison gas had been invented and were being used for the first time. Some of the fiercest battles raged along the border between Germany and France, where millions of soldiers fought from trenches dug in the muddy earth. Giant German dirigibles called zeppelins roamed the skies over England and bombed cities and towns in the dark of night, killing civilians.

In the north of Italy, the powerful Austrian army was locked in combat with Italian troops. Battles raged through towns and cities and many houses were destroyed by artillery. By this time Roncalli was again teaching in the seminary, but his students became fewer and fewer as more and more young men went into the army to aid in the defense of their country. In the spring of 1915, Roncalli himself was again called into military service as a sergeant to take up duty as a nurse for the wounded.

Once again he accepted his duty cheerfully and plunged into his military work with zest and enthusiasm. He grew a full, thick, military mustache to go with his uniform. Again, he was stationed at Bergamo, and he worked long hours caring for the wounded who had been sent there from the battlefields. The Italians had suffered a ter-

*This illustration shows the German Zeppelin blimps roaming the skies over England. Right, Roncalli as a sergeant in the Italian Army, in 1915.*

rible defeat at Caporetto and there were not enough hospitals in the north of Italy to admit all the wounded. They had to be placed on pallets in the churches in many towns and cities such as Bergamo, and there were not enough supplies of medicine. Roncalli lived daily amid the signs of horror brought on by the war. All around him lay wounded men, crying aloud in pain and dying for lack of adequate medical care.

In 1916, all the clergy in the Italian army were made chaplains and promoted to lieutenant. Shortly after his promotion, Roncalli was transferred to the battlefields, where he lived in a nightmare of death. He traveled about in bloodstained clothes, amid the sounds of guns thundering in his ears, caring for the wounded and granting the last rites of the church to the dying. For him sorrow hung heavy, like a cloud, everywhere. Many years later he recalled those terrible days, and realized that he had learned much about the human heart and spirit in these confrontations with death.

In 1918, the American, British, and French forces won a series of smashing victories over the Germans and by November the enemy agreed to accept an armistice with terms dictated by the victors. The bloodiest war in history until that time had come to an end, and the world breathed a sigh of relief.

Angelo Roncalli once more put away his uniform and returned to teaching at the seminary in Bergamo. The terrible war had disillusioned many young people in Italy, who wondered what life was all about when civilized men killed each other in the streets and bombed the homes of innocent people.

Their restlessness worried Roncalli, and he knew he must work harder than ever if he was to give these youngsters hope and faith in the future. As he saw them forming into gangs and fighting among themselves, he realized how bitter they must feel.

Roncalli saw that the youths in Bergamo needed something to take them off the streets, so he took what little money he had saved from his military pay and established a youth center. It was called a student house, and it provided a place for young Catholics to meet and talk, study, and have recreation. There were sleeping quarters for young men on the second floor of the building.

The idea caught on immediately, and the young people soon flocked to the student house. They liked the jolly, witty priest who ran it, because he didn't preach to them in a sanctimonious way. He listened to their problems, engaged in lively debate with them, loaned them small amounts of money, and most of all, inspired them with the example of his own faith and goodness.

In addition to these duties, the tireless priest was spiritual director of the seminary and the leader of several other organizations. At night, he worked on a book about St. Charles Borromeo.

Occupied as he was with all these activities, Roncalli hardly had time to think about what might be the next phase of his career in the church. In fact, he felt happy with the good he was accomplishing and the people he was helping. He had no way of knowing that more changes in his life were coming within the next two years.

_This illustration shows the battlefront during World War I. At this time Roncalli was a chaplain with the rank of lieutenant, and daily he lived among the grimmest horrors he would ever know._

# Toward Broader Horizons

Angelo Roncalli hadn't forgotten the teachings of Bishop Radini-Tedeschi, and as he went about his priestly duties he often asked himself if this were the way the bishop would have done it. He wanted to succeed in all his endeavors in Bergamo, because this was Radini-Tedeschi's city. He was very pleased to hear that the Pope described Bergamo as the most Catholic city in Italy, because he knew the bishop would have been pleased.

One day in November of 1920, as Roncalli sorted the day's mail, he suddenly paused, staring at one from Rome. He opened it quickly. It was from Cardinal van Rossum. He read its contents silently and frowned deeply in thought, then read the letter again. It said that Pope Benedict XV, who had succeeded Pope Pius X, had requested that the cardinal write Roncalli to ask if he would be willing to come to Rome. If so, he would be appointed director of the Society for the Propagation of the Faith in Italy, an important church post. There was no denying the honor of the offer. By accepting this post, Roncalli would be in an excellent position for future promotion within the church organization.

Another man might have been delighted, but the letter filled Roncalli with something akin to sorrow and regret. He did not want to leave Bergamo nor his student house. He had much to do—a lot of work had to be done—and the numerous projects he had undertaken were far from finished. There was so much good he could accomplish in Bergamo. How could he leave now?

He sought the advice of his friends, but his questions were always met with the same reply—he should go to Rome without question. It was God's will.

Roncalli did not understand why he had been selected. It might have come

---

*Roncalli appears in this picture standing behind a bishop (who is wearing a biretta). This photograph was taken in 1919, when Roncalli was a teacher of theology at the seminary in Bergamo.*

about because of his excellent speeches at the Eucharistic Congress that had recently been held in Bergamo, or because of the fine work he had done in helping to organize the congress. Had this attracted the attention of the Holy See? He had no answer. He was stunned and surprised, but decided he could not refuse a request that had been made by the Pope himself. So once more he packed his meager belongings and set out for the Vatican and his new job.

He arrived for work in January of 1921, and soon learned that his task would be a very difficult one. The Pope asked to see him immediately. After the traditional formal greeting, the Holy Father advised Roncalli of what was expected of him. He was asked to completely modernize every national Society for the Propagation of the Faith to increase their effectiveness. He was to visit every important center in Italy and the rest of Europe and revamp the entire organization. This was to be done, he was told, without offense to the older, more conservative members of the societies. It was to be a delicate diplomatic task, to be handled with great tact. It would take a likable man, and Roncalli certainly qualified.

Roncalli plunged into the job and worked hard at it, but the next year Pope Benedict XV died. Roncalli wondered what the new pontiff, Pope Pius XI, would think of the changes in the societies. At the first opportunity Roncalli expressed his great enthusiasm about the task the late Pope Benedict had given him. The new Holy Father not only approved of the idea of con-

tinuing the task, but also made other changes in the societies' structure. He promptly elevated the societies to the rank of a pontifical institution. This meant that the national societies would no longer be entirely independent of each other. Each one would now be an autonomous organization but would report to the main headquarters in Rome.

To arrange this new organization of the societies, Roncalli traveled widely. He found himself in Vienna, Aachen, Paris, Munich, Lyons, and Brussels. His work as a diplomat was remarkable. The situation in France was especially delicate since there were two societies for the Propagation of the Faith, each with disdain for the other.

Somewhat doubtful as to his chances for success, Roncalli approached the heads of both French societies. Carefully he told them that moving the headquarters to Rome would clearly show how important both societies were to the Vatican.

When they objected strenuously, Roncalli said that he understood their fears and sympathized with them. He then gave each of them the opportunity to present his side of the question. Then he set about to allay their fears, point by point, assuring them repeatedly that the societies would not lose importance in the reorganization. His obvious sincerity and respect for their positions eventually won them over, and the move of the headquarters to Rome was accomplished with very little friction. Roncalli had handled a difficult diplomatic situation with brilliant tact.

---

*Roncalli traveled widely through Europe in his capacity as director of the Society for the Propagation of the Faith in Italy. Among the cities he visited were Vienna, Paris, and Brussels.*

*Aerial view of Vatican City, seat of the Roman Catholic church. St. Peter's Basilica, with its famous dome, dominates the center of the city.*

Pope Pius XI declared 1925 a Holy Year, and thousands of people from all over the world prepared to visit Rome for the observances. Someone had to handle the tremendous task of arranging hotel accommodations for all of these people, setting up schedules, attending to transportation problems, and handling a thousand other details. The Pope had been so impressed with Roncalli's ability that he now called on him to oversee this task.

Once again Roncalli was equal to the job. The Holy Year observances were conducted effectively and Roncalli seemed to be everywhere at once, attending to details and working long hours. He even found time during the year to accept the position of professor of Patristics—the study of the writings and lives of people important in the history of the church—at the Seminario Romano where he had once been a student.

When the preparations for the Holy Year ended and the Pope realized just how fine a job Roncalli had done, he knew that this man was needed on a higher plane within the church organization. The Roman Catholic church often has trouble finding able administrators, and when a man with Roncalli's organizational talents and amiable personality comes along, the Holy See wants to be certain that these abilities are not wasted.

Monsignor Eugene Tisserant, who had been dealing diplomatically with Bulgaria, had suggested to Pope Pius XI that an apostolic visitor be named to that country. The apostolic administrator of the Roman Catholic church in Sofia, the capital of Bulgaria, had recently died, and the problems of Catholics in that country had been thrown on the Pope's shoulders. The apostolic visitor would have diplomatic status with the Bulgarian government and would act as a liaison between the Roman Catholic church, which had a very small membership, and the Bulgarian Orthodox church.

Angelo's friends and family paint his archbishop's coat of arms on the wall of the Roncalli home. They were all very proud of Angelo's accomplishments.

The Pope considered the request carefully. Most of the population of Bulgaria belonged to the Bulgarian Orthodox church, which did not recognize the Pope as its leader but was still closely identified with the Roman Catholic church in its beliefs and practices. The Vatican had always tried to remain on friendly terms with the Bulgarian church, and hoped that someday the two groups could again be joined. The two churches, however, did have their differences, and it would require diplomatic skill and tact to deal with the Bulgarians. There could be no better choice for the post than Roncalli, the Holy Father decided.

The title of archbishop of Areopolis was conferred upon Roncalli, since as a representative of the Pope in a foreign land he would need some official Vatican recognition in order to give him influence in diplomatic circles. The next day he celebrated his first Mass as an archbishop, and his parents were present for the momentous occasion.

Roncalli packed hurriedly, anxious to move to Bulgaria and take on his new challenge. But there was one thing he wanted to do before leaving the country: go home to Sotto il Monte for a few days to visit his family and lifelong friends.

It was a lovely spring day when he arrived in the little mountain village and approached his father's farmhouse. Around him the fields were budding and green blades of grass sprouted everywhere. He smelled the freshly plowed earth of the farm and welcomed the simplicity of a peasant's life once more. Although he now held the solemn, dignified title of archbishop, Roncalli was still the same happy, outgoing person he

had always been. He had always said that a sad priest was a bad priest, and the same held true of an archbishop, he believed.

News of his homecoming traveled rapidly through the tiny village, and soon all his friends and relatives came around to see him. They sat on the wide, old front porch of the farmhouse, laughing and recalling old times. Though awed with Angelo's high rank in the church, they were so happy to see him that they soon relaxed. Once again he was just Angelo Roncalli whom they loved, and they were amused by his quick wit and his lack of aloofness. The kindness and understanding he had always shown touched all of them.

They laughed about his lazy, easy-going boyhood when he used to stop and play along the walk to and from school. Some of the older townspeople confessed that they would never have predicted that he would someday rise to a position of eminence in the church. Angelo laughed with them and admitted that he certainly had gotten off to a slow start as a student.

As archbishop, Roncalli had selected a coat of arms, which was traditional. He chose a round tower on a field of red with white crossbands. Below the coat of arms was inscribed his motto, *Obedientia et Pax*, which means "Obedience and Peace." Later his family and some of his friends painted his coat of arms on the wall at home and gazed at it with a deep sense of pride.

It was the kind of warm homecoming that Angelo Roncalli was to cherish for the rest of his life. Bolstered in heart and spirit, he lingered no longer in the past nor the present, but turned toward his future in Bulgaria.

# Mission in Bulgaria

Bulgaria and its capital, Sofia, were bathed in sunlight when Angelo Roncalli arrived in April, 1925. But despite the warm spring weather and the new green leaves that had begun to appear on the trees, there was an ominous air of violence.

Bulgaria was a poor country, and one that was torn by dissenting groups of desperate people. King Boris III was the ruler of the nation but his government had violent opposition from groups who wanted a different kind of government. Only nine days before Roncalli arrived, terrorists had set off a bomb during the funeral of Prime Minister General Kimon Gheorgiev. Terrorists had murdered the Prime Minister, but they were not content to stop at that. The bomb exploded in a huge Orthodox cathedral, killing nearly 150 people and injuring more than 300 others.

The government reacted to the bomb blast by severely restricting the people. Many citizens were arrested on the slightest suspicion of favoring the terrorists, and shot by police firing squads. Families were separated as people were taken to jail, sometimes never to be seen again.

This was the atmosphere of violence and unrest in Bulgaria when Roncalli arrived. The religions of the country were also divided and there was suspicion and distrust between the Orthodox church and the Roman Catholic church. Education was poor and widespread poverty kept most people in their own villages, struggling to survive and remaining ignorant about other people and other places. The two religions were prejudiced against each other, for they had little knowledge of the similarities in their beliefs.

---

*Terrorists bomb a Bulgarian Orthodox church during the funeral of Bulgaria's Prime Minister. He had been killed by terrorists. This disaster occurred only nine days before Roncalli arrived in Bulgaria.*

In Roncalli's first sermon in the capital city, he urged Roman Catholics to forget these prejudices against their "separated brothers" and to take definite action in their everyday lives to prove their love for their fellow men. Too often, he pointed out, people dislike other human beings simply because they are of a different race, religion, or political belief. This negative attitude makes life harder for everyone in the country, he declared. Times were hard enough without adding to the troubles.

Always a man of action, Roncalli knew that sermons in the churches were not enough. The best way to understand the problems facing him was to get out and visit people all over the country. In the 1920's, roads were bad in Bulgaria, but a few automobiles were available for long distance travel. Roncalli hired one of these and began a long journey through Bulgaria's mountains, valleys, and hilly farm country. All along the way he visited churches and sought out Catholics with whom he could talk. Over and over again, he urged them not to give up hope and faith in God even though times were bad.

Along the route, especially in such cities as Svilengrad and Adrianople, Roncalli's heart sank as he saw the empty churches that had been abandoned by their congregations. The political violence and the feeling of hopelessness had driven many Bulgarian Catholics away from their habit of regular worship.

Through it all, however, rode Roncalli, his rotund form bouncing about in the rickety car that rattled over the

almost impassable, deep-rutted roads. When the car could go no farther on the roads, he borrowed a horse from a farmer and continued on horseback. The peasant farmers he met were amazed to see so high a church dignitary out in the country, visiting them. And they were even more amazed to find him on horseback, rather than in a fashionable carriage.

Even the weather seemed to be against Roncalli as he traveled from town to town. Great torrents of rain poured down in needle-like streaks, drenching him and turning the dirt roads to mud. One night he slept in an abandoned church on some straw matting as the rain poured down on the leaky roof.

His journey caused many country people to take heart. Here was a high-ranking official of the church who thought enough of them to endure hardship to visit them. Roncalli, in turn, was impressed with what he learned on the journey. To help these people, he realized, would require more than handouts and blessings. As well as spiritual encouragement, the Catholics of Bulgaria needed greater opportunities to earn a living. Since the Orthodox people ruled the country and controlled the economy, it would be necessary to work diplomatically with them in an effort to win better opportunities for Catholics.

It took several years for Roncalli to earn the respect and trust of the Orthodox leaders, but he succeeded. They were impressed with him as a man of simple faith who sincerely desired greater friendship between the two religious groups. As a result of his urging, the diplomas granted by Catholic schools were finally recognized by the government. This made it possible for Catholics to get better jobs and earn higher wages. Roncalli also founded the first Catholic seminary in Bulgaria and encouraged the construction of new schools and churches throughout the country.

He accomplished all this in the early 1930's, at a time when most of the world was in deep trouble. The economies of the major countries had been plunged into a depression after the stock market crash of 1929 in the United States. Industries could not find enough customers for their products, so they could not employ workers. Millions of people in the United States alone were out of work and had no way to earn money to buy food for their families. Industrialists such as Henry Ford, who had built a giant manufacturing empire after inventing an inexpensive automobile for the average man, had no choice but to lay off workers. Long lines of unemployed people formed at government distribution centers to get food for their families.

The American people grew impatient when the situation did not improve after two years, and they elected a new president, Franklin Delano Roosevelt, over the incumbent Herbert Hoover. Roosevelt immediately instituted new programs to help the country, but only a little progress was made at first. Young, jobless men were put to work at jobs which would not result in the production of more consumer goods. They built roads, cleared forests, and engaged in other projects. While doing this, they lived in government camps and received food and a small amount of pay.

In Italy, some people wanted a communist or socialist government and others wanted a strong leader who would tell the people what to do, rather than have them vote as in a democracy.

*This illustration shows a church being built in Bulgaria. While Roncalli was apostolic delegate to that country, he had many schools and churches built for the Catholic population.*

Democracy, to them, seemed inefficient because people with different opinions were forever arguing about them, so some young people wanted to give up the freedom that goes with democracy in favor of a more streamlined government. Benito Mussolini, a leader of a group called the Fascists, argued in the 1920's that he could cure Italy's troubles; he soon became head of the government.

In Germany, an ambitious man named Adolf Hitler called the German democracy a failure and said he himself could run the country more efficiently. He took office as head of the government in 1933, and became a dictator who either put his political opponents in jail or had them killed. Soon the German people were without rights and Hitler was the supreme ruler. But Hitler's ambition was to rule the world. He and his Nazi Party officials built a huge, mechanized German army and began threatening the neighboring countries in Europe. He became allied with Benito Mussolini, who had by now been dictator of Italy for several years. Democratic countries such as France and Great Britain became increasingly worried as Hitler and Mussolini threatened to make war on the rest of Europe.

In Japan, military leaders had gained control of that industrialized country and they, too, began building a huge army. They talked about invading China and other nations and controlling all of Asia.

The United States Army Chief of Staff, General Douglas MacArthur, pleaded for more money from Congress to build a bigger and better defense force for America. He was worried about the Japanese plans to conquer Asia and he knew the Philippines would be in danger. At that time the Philippines were governed by the United States, which was obligated to defend them. But Congress had little money for additional defense forces, because money was needed to help the country's sagging economy.

The grim spirit of the people was reflected in the lean, spare poetry of Robert Frost, who turned away from the romantic, pleasant poetry of earlier years. Young writers such as Ernest Hemingway wrote novels about death and man's struggle against great odds. But people found time for happiness, too, by listening to the jazz beat of musicians such as Louis Armstrong. They found inspiration, too, in the example of people like Helen Keller. She had been blind, deaf, and dumb since childhood, but had overcome these obstacles and graduated from college, then had gone on to write books and encourage handicapped people the world over.

In the midst of these troubled times, Angelo Roncalli managed to inspire the people of Bulgaria with his optimism, his cheerfulness, and his faith. From Rome, Pope Pius XI watched Roncalli

*Roncalli is shown here meeting with King Boris of Bulgaria. The King caused Roncalli great disappointment by baptizing his baby in the Orthodox church instead of the Roman Catholic church as he had promised.*

and his work closely, admiring his diplomacy. The jovial archbishop had even managed to earn the friendship of King Boris, although the King previously had been suspicious of the Roman Catholic church. Pope Pius was so pleased with Roncalli that he named him apostolic delegate to Bulgaria, an even higher honor than he had enjoyed up to then.

Roncalli's only setback in his relations with King Boris and his government came when the King married Princess Giovanna, daughter of King Victor Emmanuel III of Italy and herself a Roman Catholic. After Roncalli had persuaded the King to have a Catholic ceremony in Italy, the King had a second ceremony in the Orthodox church in Bulgaria, which upset Roman Catholics in both Bulgaria and Italy. Roncalli complained when the couple's first child was baptized in the Orthodox church, since it was the child of a Catholic mother, and Boris had promised before their wedding that their children would be raised in the Roman Catholic faith.

Despite these differences, however, things continued to improve in Bulgaria and the two religious denominations grew ever friendlier and more understanding of each other. Once more, through the example of his love for all men, Roncalli had been able to introduce kindness and understanding where none had existed before.

# Diplomacy in Wartime

The qualities of Archbishop Angelo Roncalli that had made him so successful in Bulgaria did not go unappreciated by the Vatican. He had handled every project to which he had been assigned over the years with great ability and tact. His hard work, his intelligence, and the example of kindness and good faith that earned him the love of the Bulgarian people made him especially valuable to the church organization.

In November of 1934, the Holy See again showed its confidence in Roncalli's ability by naming him vicar apostolic and apostolic delegate to Turkey, as well as apostolic delegate to Greece. These were more important posts than his previous ones had been, but the news of his new appointment saddened Roncalli somewhat, for he had come to feel at home among the people of Bul-

garia during his nine-year stay in their country. However, he felt that it was God's will that he take this new assignment. His many friends in both the Orthodox and Roman Catholic churches of that country were sorry to see him leave.

In his farewell address on Christmas day, 1934, which was broadcast by radio, he said that every Bulgarian would always have a special welcome at his house, wherever he may be. Tears were shed by both Orthodox and Catholic leaders when he said good-bye.

He soon found out that his job in Turkey would be more challenging. Kemal Ataturk, who headed the country's government, was against all organized religion, no matter what the faith—Mohammedan, Orthodox, or Catholic. Shortly after Roncalli arrived

---

*This photograph was taken on December 10, 1934. At this time, Roncalli was preparing to leave Bulgaria for his new post in Turkey and Greece.*

in Turkey, a law was passed prohibiting the wearing of religious garb in public. High-ranking church officials were allowed to break this law, but Roncalli decided immediately that he would obey the government's decree, in order to win the trust of government officials. This proved to be a wise decision, for the Turkish officials soon came to like and respect the new apostolic delegate.

Though Roncalli's responsibilities covered both Turkey and Greece, he established residence in Istanbul, Turkey's capital. He soon learned to enjoy the ancient city of Istanbul. He loved to walk the streets, browsing in old bookstores and antique shops. The history of Turkey and the people of the country impressed him, even though the vast majority of Turks had different religious beliefs than his own.

While in Turkey, Roncalli had only about ten thousand Roman Catholics to look after. However, he managed to institute and improve many programs. Many Catholic schools, long the finest educational institutions in Turkey, were now being forced to close because there were not enough students nor enough money to keep them operating. Roncalli worked with the schools as much as he could to try to keep them open and to

maintain their position as a viable force in Turkey. He arranged that the churches would say many of the prayers in Turkish, and he encouraged the Catholic population of the country to become more familiar with the language and customs of the country in which they lived. He himself began taking lessons in the language as soon as he arrived in the country.

He journeyed often to Athens, capital city of Greece, during this time, never forgetting his responsibilities in that country. Everywhere he went, he succeeded in winning the trust and confidence of religious and political leaders.

He found that people are remarkably alike, no matter what country they are from, and that human kindness and understanding know no national boundaries. Most of all, he succeeded in bringing mutual respect among the religious groups, and winning a greater measure of acceptance for the Roman Catholic church. By example, he showed the different religions how to live in peace together, guiding them quietly and steadily through difficult periods. In both nations, he worked unceasingly for better schools, new churches, and improvement of conditions for the poor.

---

*This illustration shows Angelo Roncalli walking among the ancient Greek ruins in Athens. He was in that city as the apostolic delegate to Greece.*

In 1936, General John Metaxas established a right-wing dictatorship in Greece which was even less friendly to Catholics than the previous government had been. New laws were passed which prevented missionary work from being carried out in Greece. Roncalli, however, was able to lessen the harshness of these laws through the use of diplomacy. The government allowed him to build a Byzantine cathedral in Athens, and the Pope made the Greeks very happy by announcing that this church would belong to a Byzantine bishop of Athens who would be responsible for Catholics in both Turkey and Greece.

During his service in Turkey and Greece, Angelo Roncalli experienced two great personal tragedies—the deaths of his father and mother. His father's death came in 1935, when Angelo was in Istanbul, but he was able to return to Sotto il Monte to spend a week with his bereaved family. His mother passed away in 1939 when he was in Greece, but this time the grim world situation made it impossible for him to leave. This was also the year in which Pope Pius XI died, and Roncalli grieved deeply at the loss of his beloved Holy Father. The new pope, a brilliant scholar named Eugenio Cardinal Pacelli, took the name of Pius XII.

It was in this year, too, that Adolf Hitler decided that his German army was big and strong enough to make its first invasion attempts on neighboring countries. In September, the mechanized German army quickly conquered Poland, killing thousands. Soon nearly all of Europe was plunged into war, and it would not be long before the conflict would spread all over the globe.

Hitler's Nazi officials and troops were brutal masters. The dictator was obsessed by the warped belief that the Jews of the world were evil and responsible for most of the world's trouble. He launched his government on a drive to murder all the Jews in Europe. Night after night his troops struck in the conquered countries as well as in Germany, rounding up all Jewish people. They were taken to horrible concentration camps and many of them were murdered in terrible ways. Many Jews, however, managed to escape to neutral countries such as Turkey.

In Istanbul, Roncalli did not hesitate to speak out against the atrocities of Hitler and the Nazis. During the war he helped to save the lives of thousands of Jewish people who escaped from Nazi-occupied countries. A shipload of Jewish children managed to escape to Turkey, but the Turkish government decided to send them back to Germany since Turkey was neutral and didn't want to offend Hitler. When Roncalli heard of this he used all his powers of persuasion to convince the Turkish government to send the ship to another neutral country which would allow the children to remain in its territory. He was successful and the children were saved.

Mussolini, the dictator of Italy, had joined his ally Hitler in the war against the other countries. When his armies invaded Greece, they at first were pushed back out of the country because

*One of Roncalli's many accomplishments in Greece was the building of a Byzantine church in Athens, shown in the illustration at left. This church was assigned by the Pope to a Byzantine bishop of Athens, a gesture which made Greek Catholics very happy.*

the Greeks fought so fiercely. But then Hitler's super-efficient German armies overwhelmed the outnumbered Greeks and conquered the nation, leaving Mussolini's troops to occupy the country.

It was a cruel, merciless occupation. Thousands of Greek workers were out of jobs in the cities, where virtually all industry was shut down. Starvation became a major problem in the country, but the occupation authorities didn't seem concerned about it.

Roncalli worked long and hard to win the trust of the occupation authorities as well as that of the embittered peasants. Together with the head of the Greek Orthodox church, he managed to arrange the shipment of food into Greece from the Allies. They were able to save thousands of lives in this way before the war ended.

The tide began to turn, and soon the forces of Hitler, Mussolini, and the Japanese military leaders were suffering large-scale defeats. Hitler had attacked the Soviet Union and his armies had killed millions of Russians and occupied large portions of that vast nation. But the Russians fought stubbornly, and eventually they were able to drive the Germans back.

In the meantime, the Japanese had launched an air attack on the American naval base at Pearl Harbor in Hawaii before declaring war. Their troops quickly overran much of the Orient and many islands in the Pacific. But they found the going tougher in the Philippines, where General Douglas MacArthur led his small force of Filipino and American troops in a brilliant defense. After several months of bitter fighting, the Japanese finally conquered the islands, but MacArthur, who had been forced to go to Australia, vowed to return and drive out the invaders.

With the great industrial might of America now in the war, Germany, Japan, and Italy went down to defeat. The occupied countries of the world were liberated. Mussolini was caught and executed by Italians and Hitler committed suicide as Germany collapsed. With these defeats, peace at last returned to the world.

It was during the final months of the war that Angelo Roncalli received an appointment to a still more important post: papal nuncio to France. The papal nuncio, unlike the apostolic delegate, is an accredited diplomatic representative of the Holy See. The Holy See had always considered France one of the most important nations as far as the church was concerned, because it was one of the most advanced countries in

*These Germans and an official of the Roman Catholic church are discussing the problem of aiding Catholics wounded in the fighting in World War II. The Catholic church believes that during a war it must aid all Catholics no matter which side they fight on.*

the world and because there was a long history of trouble for the church there. In prewar years some of the government and social leaders of that country had been suspicious of the church's influence on the people, and the French Catholics had resented the fact that they had to accept Italy as the headquarters of their church.

Most papal nuncios had been of aristocratic background, able to fit easily into French social life, for French leaders were very much concerned with correct social manners, brilliant conversational ability, and pride and sensitivity.

Roncalli wondered if the Vatican had made a mistake in sending a roughhewn peasant like himself on so delicate an assignment. But he underestimated his own qualities that had earned him the love and respect of men in many different countries. Actually, his education had taken him a long way from his days as a peasant boy. He was well versed in literature, music, art, history, and politics, and he combined this knowledge with great wit and an engaging personality—though he still spoke French with the harsh accents of northern Italy.

The Holy Father had not made a mistake in choosing Angelo Roncalli, as the years ahead were to prove.

# The Gentle Name of John

France was an unsettled nation that had just been liberated from the German conquerors when Angelo Roncalli arrived to take up his position as papal nuncio. General Charles de Gaulle, who had led the French forces in exile during the German occupation and who had returned with the American, British, and Canadian troops to liberate the country, was now president of the provisional government of France. The General was known as a cold, aloof, aristocratic man who was extremely proud and sensitive.

The church was in trouble, for it had lost a great deal of popularity and respect in France as a result of World War II. The bishops and many of the priests had ministered to German Catholic leaders and troops as well as French Catholics during the occupation. This was because the church believed that the members were its main concern, especially in time of crisis. To them, if a man was Catholic it did not matter which side of a war he was on. But many of the French men and women who had fought in the secret resistance movement against the German conquerors all during the war hated everyone in France who had been friendly with the Germans in any way.

The papal nuncio was considered to be the dean of the diplomatic corps accredited to France. On New Year's Day, the nuncio traditionally conveyed his greetings and the greetings of the rest of the corps to the president of the country. Roncalli arrived in Paris just in time to take up this official duty on January 1, 1945.

On this, his first audience with de Gaulle, Roncalli smiled and tried to be friendly, but the tall, gaunt general was as cold as ice. He bowed stiffly and said only a few very formal words of greeting. Roncalli was determined, how-

*Here we see Roncalli as papal nuncio, conveying the greetings of the French diplomatic corps to General de Gaulle on New Year's Day, 1945.*

*Roncalli is shown here on one of his walks through the streets of Paris. He especially enjoyed talking to merchants and laborers in the side streets, and the Parisians loved him for it.*

ever, and as the months rolled by he steadily gained the trust of other French leaders. Finally even de Gaulle had to admit that the Catholic bishops had acted according to their consciences and had meant no harm to France. He dropped his previous demands that a large number of bishops be sent back to Italy. Roncalli's natural sincerity and warmth was beginning to earn him the respect of the leaders of France.

Knowing that Frenchmen love good food, as he did himself, Roncalli hired the best chef he could find in Paris and began giving luncheons for political leaders, diplomats, and religious leaders. He introduced them to some of the specialties of his home region in Italy and they loved them. His gaiety, wit, and intelligent conversation at these luncheons soon made him popular with everyone who attended.

His high post in diplomatic circles entitled him to a limousine and a driver, but Roncalli liked to walk all over Paris alone, much as he had done in Istanbul. He loved to wander down little side streets and stop to talk with workers and shopkeepers. He often spent afternoons browsing in bookshops, always one of his favorite haunts. He also spent many hours gazing at the magnificent art in France's museums, and he made it a point to visit as many dioceses in France as he could. His unpretentious, friendly manner soon endeared him to all of the people.

In 1951, Roncalli was named permanent observer to the United Nations Educational, Scientific, and Cultural Organization (UNESCO). This organization was founded by the United Nations in an attempt to aid the underdeveloped nations in building themselves up to take their rightful place in the modern world. Even though he had so many other tasks in his position as papal nuncio, Roncalli still managed to familiarize himself with all phases of UNESCO. He also endeared himself to everyone connected with the organization, because he made it a point to get to know each and every one of them, from the highest levels to the lowest.

During the years he was in France, Roncalli went home to visit his brothers and sisters and old friends in Sotto il Monte whenever he could take time off from his official duties. He loved these visits, for he never lost the joy of being with the peasant people with whom he had grown up.

The people of Sotto il Monte had reason to be overjoyed in 1953 when Pope Pius XII rewarded Roncalli for his diplomatic success in France by making him a cardinal. It was a high honor that most priests or bishops could only dream about, and Roncalli would be less than human if he were not pleased. He was in his seventies, and this seemed the crowning point of a long career in the church. According to an old tradition, the president of the Republic of France placed the red biretta on his head as part of the ritual. The president at this time was a socialist named Vincent Auriol, who was not a religious man. But he had become such a good friend of the jovial, sincere nuncio that he wanted to perform the honor. It was a tribute to Roncalli's success in his relations with the French.

The ceremony was originally supposed to be restricted to only the necessary guests. However, the Canadian ambassador, as vice-dean of the diplomatic corps, wanted very much to attend—and the Turkish ambassador, Menemengioglu, an old friend of Roncalli from his days as apostolic delegate to Turkey, was also invited. The new cardinal also invited his brothers and some other people from his native region, all of whom made the trip to Paris to see their brother and friend receive this great honor from the church.

Not long afterward, Pope Pius XII made Cardinal Roncalli the patriarch of Venice, and he was delighted to move to the lovely old city in the north of Italy, not far from his home region. At the same time he regretted leaving France and the French people, for as in all of his other positions, he felt that his work was not nearly completed when he was called away. They hated to see him go; he had been the best-loved nuncio they could remember.

The new patriarch received a noisy, joyful welcome to Venice when he arrived. It was a beautiful spring day and hundreds of gaily decorated gondolas filled with cheering people cruised the city's canals. Roncalli's brilliant scarlet robes sparkled in the sunlight as he happily gave his blessing to the crowds. But in his first address, after a big procession, he reaffirmed his humble view of himself. He told the people that he was first and foremost a pastor and their shepherd, and that he was only a man who was lucky enough to have this new responsibility.

He was glad, too, that he could finally be a pastor. He had always said that he had had no more ambition than to be a parish priest in his native area of Bergamo, but that Providence had brought him a great deal of worldly honor. Now, he no longer had to concern himself with anything but local affairs, though he continued to read many newspapers each day.

Cardinal Roncalli worked long hours, rising at five in the morning to pray and begin a full day of activity. He made himself available to anyone who wished to see him, and people came by the hundreds. He made it a point to visit every parish in his diocese and celebrate Mass in each. At night he continued to work on the history of St. Charles Borromeo that he was writing.

During a five-year period in Venice, Cardinal Roncalli improved churches, founded thirty new parishes, built a seminary, and established a new place for the patriarchal archives. Another man in his early seventies might have taken life a little easier, but hard work was in this energetic man's nature. He felt the same responsibility to Venice that he had felt to Bulgaria, Turkey, Greece, and France. He fully expected to finish his life working hard to help the people of Venice.

Destiny once again intervened in October of 1958. The world was saddened by the death of Pope Pius XII, and Roncalli left for Rome to take part in the funeral rites and the age-old tradition of choosing a new pope. He carefully packed his *cappa magna*, the great scarlet ceremonial cape he would

*This photograph, taken on March 24, 1958, shows Roncalli arriving at the entrance to the new underground basilica at Lourdes, France, during the two-day ceremonies marking the consecration of the basilica. In the background is the fort of Lourdes.*

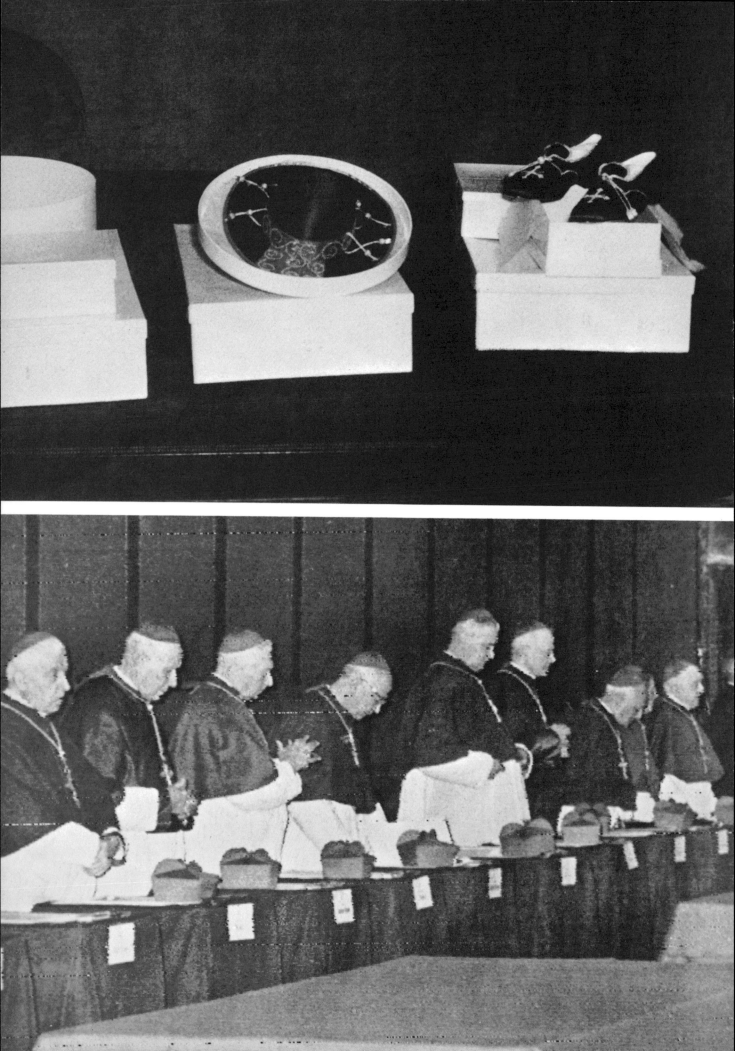

wear in ceremonies paying homage to the new pope. He fully expected to return to Venice, though, just as soon as the cardinals had selected a new pope. He even left on his desk the galley proofs of a manuscript he was writing.

All over Rome there was both sadness and excitement, as there always is when a pope dies and the world waits for his successor to be chosen. In the days that followed, nearly all of the more than fifty cardinals were arriving from all over the world. These princes of the church wore their purple robes and birettas as a sign of mourning, instead of wearing their usual scarlet attire.

Two of the cardinals who were from countries with communist governments were unable to attend the conclave. The cardinal from Yugoslavia, Cardinal Stepinac, was under house arrest in his country and was afraid to attend the conclave for fear he would not be allowed to return home. In Hungary, Cardinal Mindszenty had taken refuge in the American Embassy at Budapest. He had been told specifically by the Hungarian government that he could not go to Rome for the conclave.

Following the elaborate funeral and burial of Pope Pius XII, the cardinals stayed to take part in the traditional conclave to elect a new pope. This would begin shortly after the *Novendiali*, the nine-day mourning period for the pope, had ended. The cardinals were forbidden to discuss the coming election among themselves, but there was the inevitable speculation, both in Rome and throughout the world, about the possible candidates.

The newspapers of Rome and the other cities of the world carried many articles about the cardinals most likely to be elevated to the position of supreme pontiff. Roncalli's name was mentioned along with others, but when asked about this, he reminded people

*Top, hats and shoes which Pope John XXIII would be wearing in his official duties. Bottom, the cardinals of the Roman Catholic church stand in their places in the Sistine Chapel, waiting to start the conclave which elected Angelo Roncalli to the papacy.*

of the old adage that he who enters the conclave a pope comes out a cardinal—meaning that anyone who thinks he may be elected pope will probably remain a cardinal.

According to custom, the cardinals met in the Vatican, sometimes for several days, to vote for the new pope. Everyone who would be involved in the workings of the conclave, from the cardinals to the elevator operators, was locked inside the Vatican Palace. None of them would be allowed to leave, nor would anyone be allowed to enter, until a pope had been selected. The only contact with the outside world would be a smokestack rising above the Sistine Chapel, where the cardinals would meet to vote on the new pope.

Thousands of people gathered in St. Peter's Square to watch the smokestack. If the smoke from the stack comes out in black puffs it means that no decision has yet been reached, since the ballots are burned with wet straw. If a white puff of smoke is sighted, however, it is the signal that a new pope has been elected, for then dry straw is used in burning the ballots. The cardinals vote twice a day, once in the morning and once again in the afternoon, after they have had a chance to reconsider their individual choices for pope.

For days, only black puffs of smoke climbed into the air. The cardinals seemed unable to agree on a candidate as they repeatedly voted and sought the guidance of God in their choices. Ten times the crowd outside saw the black smoke, though twice the smoke at first looked white, causing premature excitement and cheering within the

_Black smoke rising from the chimney of St. Peter's tells the waiting crowd (shown at far left) that the Sacred College of Cardinals has not yet selected a new pope._

crowd. Then came the eleventh ballot.

Inside the Sistine Chapel, with its classic art surrounding the members, the votes came in and were read aloud by the scrutators—the cardinals assigned to count the ballots. One name began to be repeated over and over again: Roncalli, Roncalli, Roncalli.

Angelo Roncalli sat silently with the other cardinals, listening to the sound of his name again and again. His face grew white as he sat, realizing finally what was actually taking place. He could hardly believe it, and he trembled with fear at the awesome thing that was happening. A simple man of peasant background like himself? It seemed impossible.

Then the voting was ended and the final tally was made. Cardinal-Dean Tisserant walked across the floor to Roncalli and asked him in Latin if he accepted the election, made canonically, of himself as supreme pontiff.

There was a moment of silence and the usually jolly, rotund cardinal sat white faced and solemn. When he spoke he admitted that he trembled and was afraid because he felt he was insignificant in the face of such an awesome decision. But he went on to say that he accepted the election after seeing the vote, for he considered it to be God's will.

Above each cardinal's seat was a canopy with his name on the front, in plain sight. As Roncalli finished speaking, each cardinal pulled a cord at his chair and the canopies lowered until only one name remained in sight: Roncalli.

Tisserant then asked what the new Pope wished to be called. When Roncalli answered "John" there was a murmur of surprise among the cardinals. There had been no Pope John for more than 550 years, since the election of the last one, in 1410, had been held invalid.

But Roncalli explained that he considered it a sweet name and a gentle name, and that it reminded him of John the Baptist. He also pointed out that it was the name of his father and the name of the church in which he had been baptized.

When he finished speaking, Monsignor Alberto di Jorio, who was secretary of the conclave, knelt in front of him and offered him the white skullcap of the pope, the zucchetto. The new Pontiff removed his own scarlet cap, the sign of a cardinal, and put it on di Jorio's head, signifying that di Jorio would be elevated to cardinal at the next consistory.

Placing the white zucchetto on his own head, he rose and went to the altar to pray. The cardinals watched as Pope John XXIII asked God for strength and wisdom to carry out his new responsibility.

Outside, a puff of white smoke trickled upward into the sky and the cheers of thousands of people rang across St. Peter's Square.

---

*A young priest in the crowd in St. Peter's Square cheers enthusiastically as he hails the newly elected Pope John XXIII, on October 28, 1958.*

# That Which Unites

It has been speculated that Angelo Roncalli was elected pope because he had a middle-of-the-road philosophy about the role of the church today. There were two groups of cardinals: those who favored a modernization of church practices to bring them more into line with life in the twentieth century, and the conservatives who resisted change in the methods of the church. Since neither group could agree with the other on the approach the church should take, many observers feel that the cardinals settled on an "interim pope"—an elderly man who was respected by all the church officials but whose reign would be short while the conservatism vs. modernism question was being settled. Whether this speculation is true or not, Pope John XXIII quickly proved that he was not content just to heal arguments and maintain the status quo. Throughout his years of service to the church, he had always been a man of action. He had no intention of changing now, nor of doing less than his best as pope.

The first evidence of this came when he sat on the papal throne and the cardinals, true to age-old Catholic tradition, came forward to kiss his hand and foot as a sign of obedience and respect. He stopped the first one from kissing his foot and, instead, hugged him and gave him the Italian "kiss of peace" on the cheek. He saw no reason for maintaining the tradition so he ended it then and there.

Another tradition had been for the pope to dine alone. For a warm, friendly man who had always been surrounded by relatives and friends, this seemed intolerable. After several days of doing it, Pope John announced, "I can't find anything in the Scriptures that says the pope must eat by himself. From now on I'm going to have company when I eat my meals." And he promptly began inviting people to dine with him.

Not long afterward the new Pope surprised everyone again by announcing that he was going to increase the number of cardinals by naming twenty-three new ones in various parts of the

*Pope John blesses the crowd in St. Peter's Basilica as he is carried through the halls of the church during coronation ceremonies on November 4, 1958.*

When Pope John learned that he was to be visited by Mrs. Jacqueline Kennedy in 1962, he went to great pains to make certain that everything would be in order at their meeting. He was very anxious to meet Mrs. Kennedy, but was worried because he was unfamiliar with American customs.

Calling his advisers to him, he asked them many questions about the United States. The pope was especially concerned over how one addresses the wife of the president of the United States. He was also a bit worried about talking to Mrs. Kennedy, since he could speak no English.

His advisers hastened to reassure him on the language problem. They pointed out that the plans had been to speak in French at the audience, since Mrs. Kennedy spoke that language fluently. The advisers also told Pope John that it would be quite permissible to call her "Madame Kennedy" or simply "Madame." They said that the Americans called her "Mrs. Kennedy."

Pope John frowned a bit, thought about it, and then tried it out. "Mrs. Kennedy," he said. Shaking his head he said, "Madame." Then, "Madame Kennedy." Then he said no more.

When the time came he waited patiently in the room where he was to receive the President's wife. Finally the lovely young woman appeared in the doorway, and, as tradition demands, knelt there to be received by the Holy Father. Completely forgetting his earlier concern over this problem, the Pope got up, threw open his arms, strode across the room, and greeted his visitor with "Jacqueline!"

Pope John stands on the balcony of St. Peter's and blesses the crowd in the square. In the background are the other buildings of Vatican City.

world. The new cardinals included the first Negro ever to be named, Bishop Laurian Rugambwa of Tanganyika.

Things were indeed happening at the Vatican. For the first time in memory, the stale atmosphere of unchange that tradition had wrought was being brightened. The Catholic world buzzed with excitement and the newspapers ran articles speculating on what Pope John would do next. His down-to-earth human warmth appealed to common people everywhere, and his intelligence and original thinking appealed to church officials both of conservative and moderate persuasions.

People everywhere suddenly realized that there was much more to Pope John than a jolly disposition. He had his own ideas on how to make the church's message more effective in this changing age of mass communications. He had original thoughts on how the teachings of religion should be brought to all people —Catholics and non-Catholics alike. Words of faith that had been unchanged for centuries could not reach people very effectively today, he felt. Pope John reasoned that the church's message was every bit as important today as it had always been, but that communications between the clergy and the faithful had to be improved. He wanted simple, straightforward words used wherever possible.

When Pope John was apostolic delegate to Turkey, he had arranged for the part of the Mass not said in Latin to be said in Turkish. But now he eliminated much of the Latin from the ritual and Masses began to be celebrated in local

*Right, this page: the first Negro cardinal, Laurian Rugambwa of Tanganyika, receives his hat from Pope John. Far right, top: Pope John chats with an old schoolmate, seventy-seven-year-old Achille Micheletti (kneeling) and Msgr. Mario Bosio. Bottom: a little girl from Castel Gandolfo presents peaches to the Pope at that city's peach festival.*

Traditionally the pope has led a secluded life in the Vatican and has been surrounded by so many assistants and servants that he has been called "the prisoner of the Vatican."

Shortly after Pope John's election it became apparent that he was not going to fit into this tradition. The curious, impetuous pontiff would often startle the Vatican staff by suddenly departing on a solitary walk around the buildings and grounds—and sometimes even out into the streets. His love of humanity drew him into conversations with workers, merchants, and practically anybody else he met.

One day he was wandering through the palace when he came upon an electrician who was repairing some faulty wiring. The busy worker hardly noticed the robed figure that paused beside him, thinking it was one of the many priests who were staff members. John asked the electrician how his work was going and the electrician paused to answer, still not recognizing the Holy Father. He told him that his work was going quite badly and then, in a reflective way, spoke of the difficulties of supporting a large family on the small salary paid him as a Vatican employee. Salaries for employees of the Holy See had not been raised for a long time even though the cost of living in Rome had risen greatly. Some of these employees had been plunged into poverty. The man seemed resigned to this, however, and merely voiced his despair.

John listened attentively and asked more questions about the man's economic difficulties. Then he said, "We should do something about this."

"Yes, if it were possible, Father," the electrician replied.

"Just between the two of us, I am not really a priest," John told the startled man. "I am the pope."

True to his word, the pope took action shortly afterward and raised the salaries of Vatican employees by twenty-five to forty percent, the largest raises going to those who were at the bottom of the pay scale and needed the money most.

81

languages. Many people found a new and better understanding of them. New services were conducted and even new church music has begun to be composed, making use of the popular sounds and rhythms of today. None of this had seemed possible before the reign of Pope John.

In past years the pope was often called "the prisoner of the Vatican" because tradition dictated that he not venture out of its confines except on special occasions, and then only with great ceremony. Pope John saw no reason for the continuation of this custom, and he startled people by walking in the streets of Rome whenever he felt like it. He became the first Supreme Pontiff in two centuries to attend a play when he went to see a performance of *Murder in the Cathedral*, the story of the death of Thomas à Becket, who was the Archbishop of Canterbury under King Henry II of England in the twelfth century.

Pope John had always believed that "a sad priest is a bad priest." He believed that religion should be a thing of joy, and he incorporated this belief into everything he did. His audiences with people from all over the world were a source of delight to everyone who was received. He spoke in French, Spanish, and some halting English as well as Italian, and he joked and told witty stories when they were appropriate.

Once when the Holy Father decided to visit a large prison in Rome, careful security measures were taken. He was

*Pope John and aides walk across the Piazza Capranica, a small square in Rome. The Pope is waving in response to cheers by a crowd of people (not shown). Behind him is a large group of student priests.*

Far left, Pope John with Msgr. Carlo Capoferri walks to an image of Christ at Good Friday services. Left, the Pope celebrates Pentecost by reading a speech in St. Peter's Basilica.

to follow a certain route among the cell blocks, marked by a red carpet. But once inside the prison, he suddenly decided to veer off into other corridors to visit prisoners who were considered dangerous. The officials waited aghast and anxious as the Pontiff chatted with grateful prisoners and gave them hope and faith in the future.

But of all the startling changes that Pope John brought, the greatest and most far-reaching was the ecumenical spirit. When he called the leaders of the church together and told them he wished for unity and cooperation among all the Christian churches, he set in motion a whole new attitude among Christians everywhere. Leaders of Protestant, Orthodox, and Catholic churches agreed that there was a danger of losing touch with people in a modern world where materialism seemed more important than religion. His call for unity was greeted with greater enthusiasm than he had ever imagined.

The Pope's often-expressed wish to seek "that which unites men, rather than divides" caused a radical change in thinking everywhere. Famous statesmen, religious leaders, and common people from all religions—even agnostics and atheists—came to visit him. De Gaulle of France, the Prime Minister of Japan, President Sukarno of Indonesia, the President of Turkey, the Queen of England, and Presidents Dwight D. Eisenhower and John F. Kennedy of the United States came to call on this beloved Pope. They came away enchanted with his sincerity and tolerance for all the people of the world.

Pope John was now in his eighties, and he knew he could not hope to see take place all the changes he wished to enact. But he was secure in his faith that the results of the Ecumenical Council he had called would be fruitful in the years ahead. Long after he was gone, he knew, the Christians of the world would continue coming closer together in greater understanding, for he had seen this new warmth of spirit between them during and after the council.

*Above, the Pope talks with prisoners in Regina Coeli prison in Rome. Right, the Pope waves from an open car as a procession moves through the streets of Loreto. The Pope is visiting the shrine located there.*

In the spring of 1963 he was stricken by a bleeding ulcer, and though his condition improved for a short time, it soon began to grow steadily worse. He refused to let his illness deter him, however, and continued to work as hard as ever when he could. His doctors continually had to urge him to get more rest.

Finally, on June 3, 1963, death came to the beloved Pontiff, after a few days of intense suffering. He knew he was dying, but he accepted God's will without fear—as he had always done—and he was able to have a last visit with his brothers and sister to reminisce about their childhood.

When the sad news was broken to the world, more people grieved for him than had ever done so for a world figure. People everywhere wept for a man they loved, as well as for the death of the supreme pontiff of the Roman Catholic church.

The Pope's body was dressed in the traditional papal robes and carried across St. Peter's Square to the Basilica while thousands watched in silent sadness. He was buried beneath the altar of St. Peter's, and later moved to the cathedral of St. John Lateran, for he had expressed the wish that this be his final resting place.

Thousands of tributes flowed in from all over the world, including beautiful ones from leaders of non-Catholic churches. In them they expressed the hope that in the years to come, Pope John's dream of Christian unity would be realized. No greater honor could be paid to this man whose destiny was to promote understanding throughout the world, and whose goal was to seek that which unites men, rather than divides.

*Vatican Noble Guards stand at attention next to Pope John's body during the burial services at St. Peter's on June 6, 1963.*

# Summary

Angelo Roncalli seemed an unlikely person to become a world leader and head of the largest church in Christendom. Down through history there had been many popes who were brilliant statesmen, eminent theologians, and authoritative leaders; these were men who had impressed the world with their intellect, social graces, and eloquence.

To many people, Angelo Roncalli seemed to be a round, jolly peasant priest, a sort of diamond in the rough whose future would hardly lie in the most influential and crucial post in the Christian world. Yet destiny took him there, and he went on to have a greater influence in the world during his short reign than many of his predecessors had had during many years in the post.

He brought hope of unity and greater tolerance and understanding among Christians of all denominations when he convened the Ecumenical Council. If the world was ready for such a move toward understanding, Pope John XXIII was the man destined to make it possible. Few leaders could have impressed their sincerity and love of man on people of diverse religious beliefs to the degree that John did. His simple goodness gave him the ability to inspire people toward his worthy goals, and age-old feelings of distrust seemed to melt before his enlightened persuasion.

The ecumenical spirit that he set in motion has grown through the years since his death, along with ever-greater cooperation among Christians. History may well judge Pope John's reign as the dawn of a new era in which men and women of many religious denominations were blessed with a spirit that rose above their differences.

# Bibliography

ALGISI, LEONE. *John the Twenty-third*. Westminster, Md.: Newman, 1963.

ARADI, ZSOLT. *Pope John XXIII*. New York: Farrar, 1959.

————. *The Popes*. New York: Hanover House, 1958.

ATTWATER, DONALD (ed.). *A Catholic Dictionary*. New York: Macmillan, 1954.

BALDUCCI, ERNESTO. *John "The Transitional Pope."* New York: McGraw-Hill, 1965.

BERNHARD, JACOB. *The Vatican As a World Power*. New York: Longmans, Green & Co., 1939.

BOYER, CHARLES. *Christian Unity*. New York: Hawthorn Books, 1962.

CAPOVILLA, LOUIS. *The Heart and Mind of John XXIII*. New York: Hawthorn Books, 1964.

CLAUDEL, PAUL. *I Believe In God*. New York: Holt, Rinehart & Winston, 1963.

CRONIN, JOHN FRANCIS. *The Social Teaching of Pope John XXIII*. Milwaukee, Wisconsin: Bruce, 1963.

DANIEL-ROPS, HENRI. *The Second Vatican Council*. New York: Hawthorn Books, 1962.

DAWSON, CHRISTOPHER. *The Making of Europe*. New York: Shud & Ward, 1950.

DVORNIK, FRANCIS. *The Ecumenical Councils*. New York: Hawthorn Books, 1961.

FALCONI, CAROLO. *Pope John and the Ecumenical Council*. Cleveland, Ohio: World, 1964.

FESQUET, HENRI (ed.). *Wit and Wisdom of Good Pope John*. New York: P. J. Kenedy, 1964.

GROPPI, UGO. *Above All a Shepherd*. New York: Kenedy, 1959.

HALECKI, OSCAR. *Pius XII*. New York: Farrar, Straus & Cudahy, 1956.

HALES, EDWARD. *Pope John and His Revolution*. London: Eyre, 1965.

HATCH, ALDEN. *A Man Named John*. New York: Hawthorn Books, 1963.

HUGHES, PHILIP. *A History of the Church*. New York: Shud & Ward, 1935.

JOHN, ERIC. (ed.). *The Popes*. New York: Hawthorn Books, 1964.

JOHN XXIII, POPE. *Journal of a Soul*. New York: McGraw-Hill, 1965.

―――. *Mission to France*. New York: McGraw-Hill, 1966.

KAISER, ROBERT. *Pope, Council and World*. New York: Macmillan, 1963.

KLINGER, KURT (ed.). *A Pope Laughs*. New York: Holt, Rinehart & Winston, 1963.

MACGREGOR-HASTIE, ROY. *Pope John XXIII*. New York: Criterion, 1961.

McGURN, BARNETT. *A Reporter Looks At the Vatican*. New York: Coward, 1962.

MORLION, FELIX A. *Freedom's Challenge and Pope John*. New York: Harper & Row, 1963.

MURPHY, FRANCIS. *Pope John XXIII Comes to the Vatican*. New York: McBride, 1959.

NCWC News Service, Washington, D.C., from 1953-1963 for statements, speeches, and sermons of Pope John XXIII.

PASTOR, LUDWIG. *History of the Popes From the Close of the Middle Ages*. St. Louis: Herder, 1923-41.

PECHER, ERICH. *Pope John XXIII*. New York: McGraw-Hill, 1959.

ROUCEK, JOSEPH S. *Central Eastern Europe—Crucible of World Wars*. New York: Prentice-Hall, Inc., 1946.

RUNCIMAN, STEPHEN. *Byzantine Civilization*. New York: St. Martin's Press, 1953.

SODERINI, EDUARDO. *Pontificate of Leo XIII*. London: Burns, 1934.

SPELLMAN, FRANCIS J. *Action This Day*. New York: Scribner's, 1943.

SPINA, TONY and TAYLOR DAWSON. *Making of the Pope*. New York: Barnes and Noble, 1962.

VAN LIERDE, PETER. *The Holy See at Work*. New York: Hawthorn Books.

VON PAPEN, FRANZ. *Memoirs*. London: Deutsch, 1952.

WILLIAMS, MICHAEL. *The Catholic Church In Action*. New York: P. J. Kenedy, 1958.

# Index